Contents

A Little Light

*Short but Sweet Affirmations meant
to Empower & Inspire*

Each affirmation is
meant to be said
aloud and repeated
throughout the day.

Day 1

"I will never be extinguished."

I am not a survivor,
I have not been forgotten.
I am not a lost soldier,
forgotten on the battlefield of my mind.
I can always remember my true nature,
I will never be extinguished.

Day 2

"I am grounded in my being."

I am grounded in my being,
I have the courage to pursue my dreams.
I am brave beyond belief,
I am the spark that ignites the flame.
I am in a constantly expanding state,
I create my universe just like the Big Bang.

Day 3

"Every day is a lesson in surrendering to God."

I can bring light to the darkest corners of my mind,
I can release any trauma that I find.
I am the observer to every feeling and thought,
I can surrender what I believed to be true.
I can surmount any obstacle in my path,
every day is a lesson in surrendering to God.

Day 4

"I find freedom in just being me."

I am not afraid of other people's intentions,
I find freedom in just being me.

Day 5

"I am a way-shower that transforms all I see."

I bring peace to all that I witness,
I am a way-shower that transforms all I see.

Day 6

"I have a purpose beyond what I've known."

My life is my service to the divine,
I have a purpose beyond what I've known.

Day 7

"I am forgiven."

What was once seen as unforgivable
can now be released and given to God.

Day 8

"I am not my insecurities."

The universe is infinitely forgiving of your insecurities,
and infinitely gracious in its forgiveness.

Day 9

"My love is unconditional."

I am forgiving of all my past transgressions,
There is nothing that my love can't hold.

Day 10

"I have the courage to lead by example."

I have the courage to lead by example,
I am a soul that's in splendor and wonder.

Day 11

"I am free."

I am not a caged bird,
I am free to spread my wings.

Day 12

"I am protected by God's love and grace."

I am protected by God's love and grace,
I am safe to pursue my soul path.

Day 13

"I am in a constant state of metamorphosis."

I am in a constant state of metamorphosis,
I recognize that I can only be in this moment.

Day 14

"I hold myself in forgiving grace."

I give myself the space to make mistakes,
I hold myself in forgiving grace.

Day 15

"I am content with all that has been achieved."

I am content with all that has been achieved,
I no longer need to reach for a life outside of me.

Day 16

"I am not afraid of traveling beyond the known."

I am not afraid of traveling beyond the known,
I can always remember that there's safety in my soul.

Day 17

"I am in union with the source of all creation."

I respect every form that the universe manifests,
I am in union with the source of all creation.

Day 18

"I exist in oneness with all things."

I am in a constant state of divine remembrance,
I exist in oneness with all things.

Day 19

"I am an open channel for divine electricity."

I can allow the divine to flow through me,
I am an open channel for divine electricity.

Day 20

"I am a note being played by the one."

I can rejoin the eternal choir,
I am a note being played by the one.

Day 21

"I am abundant in all that I claim."

I am abundant in all that I claim,
I can invest in God's grace.

Day 22

"I am a guide for a world that's transforming."

I am blooming into my purpose,
I am a guide for a world that's transforming.

Day 23

"I am divinely expressing my purpose."

I hold the truth inside of me,
I am divinely expressing my purpose.

Day 24

"My soul holds the answer to any question."

I have wisdom beyond what I've been taught,
my soul holds the answer to any question.

Day 25

"My body is a manifestation of the divine."

I can control how I view my body,
my body is a manifestation of the divine.

Day 26

"I find happiness in the life that I lead."

I am worthy of feeling joy,
I find happiness in the life that I lead.

Day 27

"I am the creator of my reality."

I am not my thoughts,
I am the creator of my reality.

Day 28

"I am losing myself in love."

I am losing myself in love,
I'm seeing everything as one.

Day 29

"I can accept any adversity that comes my way."

I am in a constant meditative state,
I can accept any adversity that comes my way.

Day 30

"I am pure awareness."

I am not my body,
I am pure awareness.

Day 31

"I cannot be moved by another's will."

I am like a mountain,
I cannot be moved by another's will.

Day 32

"I can trust my seed like nature."

I've been planted into fertile soil,
I can trust my seed like nature.

Day 33

"I feel relaxed just like the sea."

I feel a deep connection with nature,
I feel relaxed just like the sea.

Day 34

"I can relieve any bodily stress."

I am grounded in my body,
I can relieve any bodily stress.

Thank you for reading!

Please feel free to check out my other books!

Rhymes With Divine Ties

Soothe The Soul

Lost In Wonder

The Magic Of The Moment

The Heart's Call - Coming Home Book 1

Leave Fear Behind - Coming Home Book 2

Between The Words - Divine Ties Book 1

The Word Ablaze - Divine Ties Book 2

Waves Of Truth - Divine Ties Book 3

The Everlasting Sky - Divine Ties Book 4

The Divine Ties Collection

Awaken The Soul

Every review is deeply appreciated!

Leave A Review